The Wonder of
WHITETAILS

Adapted from Tom Wolpert's *Whitetail Magic for Kids*
by Patricia Lantier-Sampon

Gareth Stevens Publishing
MILWAUKEE

For a free color catalog describing Gareth Stevens' list of high-quality books, call 1-800-341-3569 (USA) or 1-800-461-9120 (Canada).

Library of Congress Cataloging-in-Publication Data

Lantier-Sampon, Patricia.
     The wonder of whitetails / adapted from Tom Wolpert's Whitetail magic for kids by Patricia Lantier-Sampon ; photography by Daniel J. Cox.
        p.   cm. — (Animal wonders)
     Includes index.
     Summary: Text and photographs introduce a North American forest animal, the whitetail deer.
     ISBN 0-8368-0858-4
     1. White-tailed deer—Juvenile literature. [1. White-tailed deer. 2. Deer.] I. Cox, Daniel J., 1960- ill. II. Wolpert, Tom. Whitetail magic for kids. III. Title. IV. Series.
     QL737.U55L36   1992
     599.73'57—dc20   92-16947

North American edition first published in 1992 by
Gareth Stevens Publishing
1555 North RiverCenter Drive, Suite 201
Milwaukee, WI 53212, USA

This U.S. edition is abridged from *Whitetail Magic for Kids*, copyright © 1990 by NorthWord Press, Inc., and written by Tom Wolpert, first published in 1990 by NorthWord Press, Inc., and published in a library edition by Gareth Stevens, Inc. Additional end matter copyright © 1992 by Gareth Stevens, Inc.

Cover design: Kristi Ludwig

Printed in the United States of America

1 2 3 4 5 6 7 8 9 98 97 96 95 94 93 92

Whitetail deer live in North America. They get their name from their large tails, which are used to signal other deer.

Whitetails have beautiful red coats in spring and summer. In fall and winter, these coats turn gray.

Whitetail deer have big, brown eyes and narrow, graceful heads. Their favorite foods are leaves, twigs, nuts, and fruit. They grasp the food with their lips and use their teeth to grind and chew.

In spring, female whitetails, or *does*, find a quiet, wooded spot.

Here they give birth to one or sometimes two *fawn*s.

Newborn fawns are very small, but they can stand up within thirty minutes of being born. The fawns nurse on their mother's milk, which helps keep them healthy during the first few weeks of life.

Newborn fawns need a lot of sleep in their first month.

If a *predator* comes near, the fawns stay very still.

After a few weeks, the
fawns follow their mother
in search of food. They are
curious about the forest.

Summer is a quiet, lazy time for whitetail deer.

They eat plenty of tender grasses and leaves.

Growing fawns like to play.
They jump and kick their
back legs and chase one
another through the fields.
This playing helps their
muscles grow strong.

The fawns learn how to behave properly by carefully watching their mother. They also *imitate* the actions of other deer as they travel with their mother through the grassy fields and forests.

By autumn, the fawns have grown quite a bit.

Now they begin to prepare for the winter ahead. They must build up stores of fat for the long months of cold weather coming up.

Whitetails now search for foods that will give them energy, such as nuts, fruit, and farm crops.

The male whitetails, called *bucks*, grow *antlers* in the summer. By winter, these antlers are quite large.

Bucks use their antlers to fight each other during *mating* season. The strongest bucks mate with the does.

Winter can be a very dangerous time for the whitetail deer.

Freezing temperatures and deep snow make travel difficult.

Whitetails *adapt* well to cold weather. Their thick winter coats protect them from the snow and wind.

In winter, there is not much food for the whitetail deer. Before the snow gets too deep, the whitetails travel away from their homes to search for food. This way, they can save the food near their homes for times when the weather is bad and the snow is too deep to travel.

In winter, the deer eat
mostly tree bark and twigs.
They also use their *hooves*
to dig in the snow for food.

Many fawns may die during long, cold winters. This is mainly because they are still so young and small. They do not have enough body fat stored up to last through a long, harsh winter.

Sometimes whitetails are attacked and killed by predators. This is especially true for the fawns. They must always be on the lookout for timber wolves, mountain lions, coyotes, bobcats, and even house dogs. All of these animals kill and eat deer.

Finally, the snow melts and it is spring again. The whitetail deer are hungry for warm, green grass.

After its first winter, this fawn becomes a *yearling*.

Sturdy little yearlings grow up to be mature bucks or does.

Glossary

adapt — to change over time to move more easily and live more comfortably

antlers — hard, branchlike growths on the heads of some animals

buck — a full-grown male deer

doe — a female deer

fawn — a young deer

hooves — hard coverings on the feet of some animals

imitate — to copy the looks or actions of something or someone

mate — to join together (animals) to produce young

predator — an animal that hunts other animals for food

yearling — an animal that is one year old

Index